Pleasant
PATHS

Pleasant PATHS

VANCE HAVNER

Kingsley Press

Shoals, Indiana

Pleasant Paths

Published by Kingsley Press
PO Box 973
Shoals, IN 47581
USA

Tel. (800) 971-7985
www.kingsleypress.com
E-mail: sales@kingsleypress.com

ISBN: 978-1-937428-74-7

First Kingsley Press edition 2018

This first Kingsley Press edition is published under license from Baker Publishing Group.

Contents

Foreword

AGAIN the writer ventures forth with a sheaf of meditations gathered here and there, on busy travels and in quiet places. These reflections have been sweet to him and he trusts they will be so to others. He has made himself be still now and then to write such things for his own soul's good. May it help some others to "prime their pumps!" But, better still, may it point us to him in whom, if we abide, we shall never thirst but ever receive and ever overflow.

V. H.

Greensboro, N. C.

Chapter 1

Pleasant Paths

THERE is something different about a path. Not a modern highway, noisy and crowded; not even a dirt road or a pasture lane; but a path, inviting the tired spirit to come apart and rest awhile. A little trail that means escape to stroll by still waters and green pastures, or deep in the woods, with birds singing from overhanging boughs.

God's way for us is often called a path in the Scriptures. It is called the path of life (Psa. 16:11), a plain path (Psa. 27:11), the path of his commandments (Psa. 119:35), an old path (Jer. 6:16). He has told us that, if in all our ways we acknowledge him, he will direct our paths (Prov. 3:6). The path of the just is as the shining light, that shineth more and more unto the perfect day (Prov. 4:18). And it is said of wisdom that "her ways are ways of pleasantness and all her paths are peace" (Prov. 3:17).

Now, the way of wisdom is simply Christ, the way, who is made unto us wisdom (1 Cor. 1:30). And the ways of Christ are pleasantness and all his paths are peace. We do not mean that the Christian experience is a charming little idyl, just a nice after-dinner stroll down by the lakeside. It has its battles, its tribulations, its trials. But there may be persecution without and pleasantness within. The Bible always gives us both sides. Both realism and romance are there. Jesus never made his way a vacation but a vocation. He challenged men to deny self, take up the cross, sell out their goods, lose their lives to find them, let the dead bury the dead. But he also told us that his yoke was easy and his burden light. His commandments are not grievous. His ways are ways of pleasantness and his paths are peace.

Let us return to another verse about paths which we have already mentioned: "Thou wilt shew me the path of life: in thy presence is fulness of joy; at thy right hand there are pleasures for evermore" (Psa. 16:11). Here we have first THE PATH. It is the path of life and that again is Christ, who is our life. It is a plain path, for he is our light. It is an old path, tried and true. He is not merely the way leading to life, he is the life here and now, and from the moment we strike that trail eternal life is ours. We do not travel the path in the hope of reaching eternal life in heaven. We are on the way of life, not to life, and he who is our life dwells in us now.

Which leads us to the second truth of our verse: "In thy presence is fulness of joy." We have not only the path, we have THE PRESENCE. The path is before us, the presence is with us. "Lo, I am with you alway"; "I will never leave thee, nor forsake thee." It would not be enough to have a path if we had not a companion and a guide, and he is both. Moreover, in his presence is fulness of joy. That makes it a pleasant path, you see. There will be plenty of hardship and trouble along the path, but the presence makes it pleasant within.

For along the path with the presence we have the PLEASURES: "At thy right hand there are pleasures forevermore." That is what we have just been saying. So wonderfully interwoven in the text are all these precious things that you cannot separate them. The path, the presence, the pleasures. "She that liveth in pleasure is dead while she liveth" (1 Tim. 5:6), but here is a way to have both life and pleasure.

Seek, therefore, the old paths and ye shall find rest for your souls. His way is a way of pleasantness and his path is peace.

Second Reading

IT was in Milo, Maine, on the banks of the Sebec River—rugged, woodsy Maine, deer-hunter's paradise—and in late October. After a round of itinerant preaching in New England I had come down with a bad throat and was convalescing. The bed was a wilderness of magazines and papers gathered to tide me over.

Now, I hadn't noticed it before, but when one has time on his hands he perceives much that generally evades him. I found that I have two ways of reading a magazine. When it is new and I have just laid hands on it, I start on the first page with full resolution to read thoroughly, mark and inwardly digest the contents. I attack the first article with concentrated serious studiousness and I generally reap a fair harvest, if it is worth reading.

But after a while, when I have pretty well covered my supply of readables and time still hangs on my hands, I pick them up again and this time I just browse. I really don't care much whether I read or not. I pick around and look into the back pages and into the nooks and corners that first escaped my serious onslaught. Even local items in the newspaper which I would have scorned to scan in my first reading claim my attention. Odd bits of news, a bit of poetry, even an advertisement, are favored with perusal; nothing is too lowly to be granted a condescending glance.

And lo, it turns out that some of my choicest tidbits are garnered on this second round. Like the "handfuls of purpose" which Boaz ordered dropped for Ruth to glean, these pickings were the cream of the crop. I found more when just browsing than when bearing down with hard resolution.

I wonder if we mortals do not sadly overrate the fruits of our boasted concentration. Do not we often gather more from leisure than when we sweatingly "apply ourselves"? It has been said that what we are when we are not trying is what we really are, and perhaps what we learn when we are not trying affects us most.

Children learn more out of the schoolroom than in it. Indeed, they should bear down on their textbooks, but what they pick up by watching us oldsters and what they glean by the wayside may mean more than what they cram in class.

Not for a moment would we discourage hard application and full attention to Bible study. But have not some of its choicest treasures come to us when we sat down just to enjoy it, when we ate its milk and honey because it was good and not in order to check on a report card? There is much in the book that escapes you if you set out to crash it by a frontal assault. As with a love letter, what is between the lines often means most. And what lover has not found that the leisurely perusal of a letter revealed secrets he could never have extracted by the first reading?

Is it not so with the Christian? Indeed, we are to watch and pray and walk circumspectly and study to show ourselves approved unto God. But have you not met some earnest souls always hard at it, stern and serious, with jaws set and eyes aglint, and yet lacking a sweetness and restfulness, their soul-strings keyed so tightly that some of them snapped—so that they had to learn to browse? And what they could never find by hard application they learned by quiet meditation. They gathered most on second reading!

Our Lord applied himself as none other has ever done. But he who went to the cross could go fishing and visit at lowly Bethany.

Learn a lesson from leisure. "Everlastingly at it" will bring you only high blood pressure and apoplexy. Learn to read both ways as you go through the book of life. What you cannot find by digging you may discover by browsing.

Chapter 3

Jesus on the Shore

"But when the morning was now come, Jesus stood on the shore"
(John 21:4).

I am always glad when, in my reading of the Gospels, I get to the resurrection. From there on to the ascension is my favorite reading ground. Jesus' sufferings are over and he is alive forevermore. Never again will he know agony and death and the grave. I revel in those interviews with his disciples. Truly, it is morning after an awful night.

Our text sets forth a glorious morning after a night of bewilderment. The poor, discouraged, confused little band of followers, led by Peter, had gone fishing, perhaps in the hope that it might rest their jangled nerves and quiet their troubled spirits. But I imagine that through that night their faces wore the marks of their inner turmoil. What did it all mean? Why had he raised their hopes so high those three wonderful years, only to leave them with all their dreams faded and broken? They could not make sense of it. But when morning came, there he was on the shore!

It was morning after a night of failure. They had fished in vain. It was a fruitless expedition, as is any venture of life when he is not along. But in our failure we are not out of his sight. In another passage we read of his walking to them on the water when "he saw them toiling in rowing, for the wind was contrary unto them." Maclaren observes that "the cause of their dismay was the means of his approach." So here a night of failure finds him waiting on the shore. He is concerned about us when we fail. He is not like those friends who are on hand when we succeed but vanish in the hour of trouble. He sought a special interview with Peter exactly because Peter had failed miserably. If you have had a bad night, morning will reveal him on the shore! "Weeping may endure for a night, but joy cometh in the morning!"

Many there be these days who are passing through one kind of darkness or another. If your faith is in him, morning will not merely bring him, he will bring the morning, for he is the Sun of Righteousness and he shall arise with healing in his wings.

The morning after death will find him on the shore.

> I shall know him, I shall know him,
> And redeemed by his side I shall stand;
> I shall know him, I shall know him,
> By the prints of the nails in his hands.

The New Testament writers did not speak of going to heaven so much as of going to be with the Lord. It is not the other shore that charms us so much as Jesus on the shore. "Today shalt thou be with me" is what cheered the dying thief more than merely going to be "in Paradise."

One other hope thrills us: the night of this age shall end, for the believer, with Jesus on the shore. It is a night, dark and dismal, and there are few watchmen who can read the meaning of it. But God's watchman assures us, "The morning cometh." That morning is nothing less than the glorious appearing of our Lord. Call us pessimists if you will; we who look for him are not looking for night, we are looking for morning! That is optimism of the highest order. And when he shall appear, we shall be like him, for we shall see him as he is.

CHAPTER 4

A Cemetery Stroll

I'VE been for a walk in the cemetery on the edge of town.
I know that you expect something very doleful after that,
but this is no graveyard gossip. In fact, I find a tour of the
tombstones refreshing. We are always talking about whis-
tling our way through the graveyard, as though it were a
fearful place of dread and gloom. It is possible to find inspi-
ration there. Why should it be a spooky haunt of ghosts and
goblins?

There is no reason why any Christian should not find
blessings in a cemetery stroll. Here the weary are at rest.
And how weary some of them were! What volumes could be
written of heartache and sorrow, of fallen castles and faded
dreams, if these graves could speak. Sometimes our ups and
downs become so important that we forget that all these
had their days too, when it seemed the universe would fall.
But it didn't fall, and it won't fall under the pressure of your
little misery and mine; so let us simmer down before we
explode. Whatever the trouble is, it shrinks up considerably
when you stroll through the graveyard. There is no calamity
so terrible that we should let it wreck us. For there is no
trouble that God cannot manage, and those that he does
not remove on this side of the grave will certainly not last
beyond it if we entrust our keeping to him. That gives the
worst of our miseries only a few years to live, so why worry?

We walk beside the graves of many who died in the Lord,
and the grave of a Christian should be a most encouraging

stimulant. Actually, what is there on earth more cheering than the resting place of the saints? Every Christian's grave is an Easter sermon, a thrilling testimony that death has been conquered, the grave defeated, and the devil crushed. For these spirits are already with the Lord. They are not sleeping there awaiting the resurrection. They are already with Christ in the first blessed round of eternal bliss. And those crumbling bodies, some so racked with agony before the spirit departed, are not really leaving us. They are awaiting the trumpet blast and that mighty transformation in the twinkling of an eye. So nothing really is lost; the spirit did not die and the body shall be raised. Save for the human grief of temporary separation, what is there depressing in a stroll by the graves of his own?

And there comes, too, that "sweetly solemn thought" that I am nearer home today than I've ever been before. How short is my pilgrimage; how long is eternity! Am I growing more like him as I near that day when I see him as he is? How circumspectly I ought to walk, buying up each opportunity because the days are evil. So much to do, so little done!

That brings another consideration on my cemetery stroll: so many of these whose bodies lie here were unprepared. Did anybody tell them of Jesus? Did they move, day in and day out, among Christians who never let them find it out? In a land of churches, did they spend their years as a tale that is told and never have one Christian invite them to go along with him to the land that is fairer than day? If graves could speak, how they could embarrass us in our fine churches some Sunday morning if all these lost souls, forever past redemption, could file into our sanctuaries and, pointing fingers of eternal scorn, remind us, "For years I walked your streets, worked beside you, did business with you, lived among you, and never did you warn me of my impending doom nor point me to your Savior!"

There is much to learn in a cemetery. And if we learn it, we shall come back from our stroll and get busy, for "the night cometh when no man can work."

CHAPTER 5

Rainy Day

I am riding through Minnesota on a rainy afternoon, headed home from the West. Once again, grace has brought me safe thus far on another long preaching trip, and my heart is mellow at the goodness of God.

Maybe it is the accumulating years, but oftener now I am wont to look back over the road I have trod and marvel at the guiding hand. Since boyhood days in Carolina, when the call to preach first stirred my heart, one has gone before, opening doors that no man can shut. I can now begin to trace some of the pattern. The passing years piece together a design that becomes clearer as the days go by.

I fear that many times I have failed to acknowledge him in all my ways, but never for a moment can I doubt that he directs my path. And when I reflect on his eternal goodness, I marvel not that it "leadeth to repentance." Certainly the goodness of God ought to humble us in tender sorrow that ever we grieve his Spirit. It ought never be necessary for chastisement to teach us the lesson that loving favor was meant to impart. If we were in our right senses, we should be so softened and sweetened by all his benefits that we should be grieved over even the slightest transgression.

How can I ever grow cold or careless when daily I see the way open before me unplotted and unplanned by human brain or hand? With all my heart I believe that if one will walk with the Lord in the light of his Word, he will never need to pull wires and resort to tricks of his own devising to make a way. I do not quarrel with the brother who feels that he must push himself forward, but far more precious to me is that simple walk of faith that sees the pillar of cloud and fire go ever on before.

How can we be ashamed of him or timid to ascribe to him the glory when he so graciously "leads his dear children along"? Why should we ever feel embarrassed to read a Bible on a crowded train? To be sure, reading it to appear pious is reprehensible beyond words. But why should we not be glad to acknowledge him as our bread and drink in the midst of a starving world? Not a day passes but he loads us with such benefits that we should weep at ever failing to declare the glories of his name.

What a secret we have in the midst of a bewildered world that we are able to say:

> He leadeth me, O blessed thought!
> O words with heavenly comfort fraught!
> Whate'er I do, where'er I be,
> Still, 'tis God's hand that leadeth me.

It is well on this kind of a rainy day to stock one's soul for another kind of rainy day that is sure to come. For "into every life some rain must fall, some days must be dark and dreary," and when they come we shall be tempted to forget all the others. But he who has cared for the hitherto will care for the henceforth.

> Be not dismayed, whatever betide,
> God will take care of you.

And remember, he loves us as much in the night as in the daylight. And even if he puts some of his children to bed in the dark, he will get them all up in the morning!

CHAPTER 6

Twelve Hours in the Day

"ARE there not twelve hours in the day?" So spake our Lord, and he was never in a hurry. He was busy but not hurried. He knew that there is always time enough to do what God wants done—and no more time is needed by anyone than that.

What gets us into a fuss and stew is being cumbered with so much that never was God's will for us. Jesus was leisurely, and though his friends once thought he was beside himself, and though the zeal of God's house consumed him, yet he never gave the impression of that feverish frenzy that so often marks some of the saints.

For the brethren do not always get the balance right. Some are dull and listless and lukewarm and others tear around in a tempest of activity. They freeze or they fry, it seems, and few there be who strike the blessed medium.

After all, God is not interested in mere quantity production. He is not impressed with our Herculean exploits and Paul Bunyan strides if they do not issue from him. Even if they do, Elijah's big day on Carmel so often brings him next day to the juniper, all played out and ready for a season with the still small voice.

I am more and more impressed that what is so often played up as "burning up for the Lord" is too often a fair show in the flesh, often earnest and honest, but ending with a crash that brings reproach upon the sacred cause. When

God allots us our mission for him, he allows time in which to perform it. He does not favor loafing, but he does not frown on resting. Our Savior's calm, peaceful journeys over Galilee with a band of plain fishermen and lowly working-men would have exasperated some of our modern church specialists, who would have rejected the twelve because they didn't have college diplomas. But, after all, that lowly group started something that has never stopped, and we moderns cannot begin to match the gait of Galilee or the pace of Pentecost.

Our Lord never wasted his time. There are other ways of wasting time than by just doing nothing. It can be wasted by doing too much. Idleness is the devil's workshop, but so is the wrong kind of busyness. The ordered life that has its springs in God, that recognizes twelve hours in the day, gets far more done than that puttering around in a fury that ends in a flop.

The Bible has plenty of verses to stir up the saints, and most of the saints need stirring. But there are just as many verses about resting in the Lord, and we do well to balance the one with the other. It was in one of the most tempestuous hours of his life that our Lord said, "My peace I give unto you." His was not a peace for rocking-chair saints under a shade tree. It was a peace that stood him and will stand us in good stead in the storm.

It is a poor song that has no rests in it, and singing it would leave us all out of breath. Of course, some saints are like the little girl at her piano practice, who explained why she was so quiet by saying, "Mother, I'm practicing the rests!" But neither do we have to tear up the piano.

Cultivate the leisure of the Lord. "Are there not twelve hours in the day?"

CHAPTER 7

Three Witnesses

I have read a sermon of John MacNeill's, that sturdy Scottish preacher of a generation ago. He was dealing with the Passover and the deliverance of the Israelites from Egypt, and he makes much of the fact that fear played a great part in that mighty episode. He reminds us that fear has always been a mighty factor in things spiritual, that "Noah, moved with fear, prepared an ark." And, of course, we know that "the fear of the Lord is the beginning of wisdom."

Yet today a shallow theology and a puny psychology would have us leave fear out of our preaching. It is one of the popular delusions that people should never be faced with the awfulness of sin and the certainty of judgment and the fearfulness of hell, but rather be pampered with dainty sermonettes that begin nowhere and end in the same place, daisy chains of sweet, scented platitudes that perfume the stench of mortal corruption. This modern transition from beefsteak doctrine to peanut-butter-sandwich theorizing has left us with a generation which grace has never taught to fear before grace their fears relieved, and, consequently, men have no heart to sing, "How precious did that grace appear the hour I first believed."

Then I read from another prince of preachers, England's great Robert Hall, who exposed for us another delusion. Another taboo among us preachers today is the old-fashioned practice of preaching against sin. Negative preaching has been sentenced to the shades of the past as a relic of antiquated psychology that flourished before there dawned this age of sweetness and light (?). But hear Robert Hall, in a charge to a young minister:

> Be not afraid of devoting whole sermons to particular parts of moral conduct and religious duty. It is impossible to give right views of them unless you dissect characters and describe particular virtues and vices. The works of the flesh and the fruits of the Spirit must be distinctly pointed out. To preach against sin in general without descending to particulars may lead many to complain of the evil of their hearts while at the same time they are awfully inattentive to the evil of their conduct.

Outlandish, do you say? Well, I shall be convinced when these who pipe against such preaching get to where they can preach like Robert Hall!

Then I picked up a word from Charles G. Finney, that American Elijah, and found another modern balloon pierced by his sharp thrust. He is speaking of excitement in religion, that bugaboo of the saints at ease in Zion:

> Many good men have supposed, and still suppose, that the best way to promote religion is to go along uniformly and gather in the ungodly gradually and without excitement. But, however sound such reasoning may appear in the abstract, facts demonstrate its futility. The state of the Christian world is such that to expect to promote religion without excitements is unphilosophical and absurd. The great political and other-worldly excitements that agitate Christendom are all unfriendly to religion and divert the mind from the interest of the soul. Now, these excitements can only be counteracted by religious excitements. And until there is sufficient religious principle in the world to put down irreligious excitements, it is vain to try to promote religion except by counteracting excitements.

Preposterous, do I hear? Well, who among us today is reaching the hearts of men as this man did?

MacNeill, Hall, Finney, in the mouths of three witnesses is great truth established: men must fear, men must face sin, men must be stirred. Our delusions have made pygmies of us. Let us hark back to the days of the giants and learn a thing or two!

"For a Season... Forever"

YOU need not hurry through the little epistle to Philemon just because it is short. Here is one of the "choicest
gifts wrapped in smallest packages."

This morning I have been intrigued with the fifteenth
verse. You remember that Onesimus had robbed his master and had run away. In Rome he met Paul and became a
Christian. Paul sent him back to Philemon, his master, with
this letter interceding for his reinstatement. As he piles up
his arguments in favor of the new Onesimus, he says, "For
perhaps he therefore departed for a season, that thou shoul-
dest receive him forever."

Now, Onesimus should not have robbed his master and
he should not have run away. Such behavior as that is not
to be defended in any day or generation. And yet, in the
providence of God, it led to his meeting Paul and becoming a Christian, so that he who left home a rebellious slave
returned a regenerated servant. It was the best thing that
could have happened, both for Onesimus and Philemon.
Even as a business proposition it was a bargain, for Paul
offered to make up the theft; and Onesimus certainly would
be a better workman saved than unsaved.

I have no theory to propound, nor am I venturing into
an ethical dissertation. I am not even interested in discussing the directive and permissive will of God as applied to
this case. I do observe that Onesimus departed "for a season"

that he might be received back "forever." At least, Paul says "perhaps." And I find in it an illustration of what I have often noticed in the ways of Providence, which are past our finding out. How often have dark chapters in our lives which, viewed alone, caused us grief and pain turned out, in the long view, to spell the difference between "for a season" and "forever." I do not mean that we may ever do evil that good may come of it. But I do perceive that in the hands of the destiny that shapes our ends, rough-hew them as we may, the believer finds one day that all things have worked together for good to the called according to his purpose.

I cannot explain it. If I could, it wouldn't be worth writing about. All that I know about it is that God who makes the wrath of men to praise him is so much stronger than the devil that he can turn the designs of the prince of darkness against the designer himself. Satan overstepped himself when Onesimus ran away. He may have caused him to run away, but God saw to it that he went to Rome and met Paul. For Onesimus was one of the called according to God's purpose, and no trick of the devil can outwit that purpose.

Perhaps as you read, you can testify to the truth of this, for you have seen it work in your own life. I think of ten lone, lean years in my own past, when I was confused and bewildered and quite out of his blessed will. Now, I should not have been in such a state, and often since I have wondered why someone or something did not jolt me out of it earlier. And yet—and yet—as I look back now, I perceive that I learned some lessons from it that I should never have known otherwise. I do not justify that careless course by the lessons it taught me. And yet I insist that Satan shall not have it all his way; there is a redeeming feature, even in those runaway years. Perhaps I "departed for a season" that I should return to remain forever.

Remember, I did not set out to explain it. I can only rejoice in the compass of God's unfailing purpose, in that love that did not let me go. And some day, by a better light, we shall perceive that even those pages that caused us shame and tears his eternal grace has bound into the volume and that he, who having begun a good work will always perform it, has seen that even when we departed for a season we should return, to be received forever.

CHAPTER 9

Riding the Local

THE big "through" train was over three hours late. There was a local going earlier. The agent said, "At least you will be able to get a seat, for it won't be crowded."

It wasn't. Nobody likes to ride the local. Disgusted passengers decided to wait or take the bus. So I had a whole seat for my books and papers.

Actually, I'm having a good time. There's something old-fashioned about riding the local. It is beneath the dignity of most Americans now. It is too slow these days, when everybody is in such a hurry—going nowhere. The local is a left-over from a more leisurely age, before streamliners saved us more time—to waste.

But there are compensations besides not being crowded. You really relax on a local—not on the fast train—because you have to. There's no use being in a hurry. You might as well take it easy, because the train certainly does; and really you can't get there before the train does. Nobody else is in a hurry, nervously looking at a watch every ten minutes, wondering whether this train will connect with one down the road. This train will never connect with anything much, so why worry?

All of which suggests an allegory. Life is like this. Almost everybody rides the fast train these days.

From cradle to grave, we live in a fever over our baggage, making connections, with speed the primary consideration.

We are all so tense getting to where we're going that few ever look out the windows as we go along.

Perhaps we might as well copy our fathers and ride a local through this world. After all, it goes through the same country and arrives at the same destination. And one is more likely to see the scenery as he goes along. Some of the passengers may be a little old-timey, but they're more leisurely and better company. They're not in such a hurry to be somewhere else that they see nothing where they are.

The awful congestion in travel these days has its counterpart in the realm of things unseen. Multitudes are hurrying to and fro, knowing little of why or where they go. Too crowded to rest, too hurried to relax, too weary to see God's splendor as they travel through, they have a miserable time. Everybody is trying to crowd into the streamliners, because everybody else is trying to do the same thing. They haven't time to stop and ask why, for if they did they'd miss a connection somewhere down the road! Of course, it would drive them frantic to ride a local. So they scramble on and end up in hospitals, insane asylums, failure and despair.

I've just learned that I can get off down the road and change to the fast train. I think I'll stay on the local. Some others have decided to stay too; we're beginning to see the difference. Maybe these days will lead us in more ways than one to find out how much better are some older, slower things.

I've noticed, too, that I have done more work on this ride than on a crowded Pullman. Is it not true of life itself?

Yes, I think that in living, as well as in today's journey, I'll ride the local.

CHAPTER 10

Can You Take a Back Seat?

MOST of us like the driver's seat. And if, somehow, life shoves us into a back seat, we like to be back-seat drivers. He is a rare soul who can behave himself graciously in life's back seat.

But it has been done. I am thinking of two men who did it, one in the Old Testament and one in the New.

Samuel was the last of the judges. He got caught in a change of dispensations. The people of Israel wanted to be like the nations around them—the first step in many a downfall. They wanted a king.

Samuel counseled against it. He knew that it was not God's best for them. But when it had to be done, he graciously took a back seat in favor of the glamorous Saul. There he remained for the rest of his days, far abler and far godlier than the king.

Time and again, in the course of things, a Saul supersedes a Samuel. Not every Samuel can step aside like this one. It is not easy to resign oneself to "servants upon horses" and "princes walking as servants upon the earth." But Samuel took his back seat and stayed in it well.

John the Baptist also took a back seat. He too was caught in a change of dispensations. As Samuel was the last of the judges, so John was the last of the prophets. For a little while his was a spectacular career. He stood beside the Jordan and called the listening multitudes to repentance. A colorful figure, he was the talk of the country.

Then Jesus came along, and soon the multitudes turned to him. When this was reported to John, he answered with a classic text for all saints of the back seat: "He must increase but I must decrease."

Not every Christian has learned to take second place, even to Jesus. How often has he taken the background while proud self has refused to resign in his favor. One may even be a minister of no small parts and a preacher of many accomplishments, but giving the impression, withal, that if he is in the back seat, he is a back-seat driver! Few there be who attain to "none of self but all of thee."

Paul summed it up best of all with "To me to live is Christ" and "Not I but Christ liveth in me."

He who so gives Christ the chief place will likewise esteem others better than himself. He will take the lower seat and be invited up higher instead of reversing the process. He will walk in the steps of him who came not to be ministered unto but to minister, and in spirit he will not be above washing the feet of the brethren. He will not be a Diotrephes loving the preeminence but a Demetrius of good report clothed with humility. And he will be a blessing to everybody, for he will have learned the Beatitude of the Background.

In a day when men climb for the ladder's topmost rung and even the saints scramble for the chief seats in the synagogue, blessed is he who can take a back seat, whether as Samuel for a lesser or as John the Baptist for a greater, even the greatest of all.

CHAPTER 11

On Snapping Out of It

IT was Richard Baxter who wrote, "I was once wont to meditate most on my own heart. I was always poring either on my sins or wants or examining my sincerity; but now I see more need of a higher work and that I should look oftener upon Christ and God and heaven than upon my own heart."

It is a good word. Most people never search their hearts, nor do they ever have a spiritual check-up. But others spend their days in a perpetual clinic, with themselves as both doctor and patient. The devil has a lot of fun with sensitive, conscientious souls given to introspection. He makes them connoisseurs of moods, specialists in self-examination, and much given, as was Richard Baxter, to examining their sincerity. They worry because they do not pray enough, read the Bible enough, testify enough, rejoice enough.

There is, obviously, a very common-sense way out of such a condition. If one really is not doing these things as he ought, the self-evident remedy is to begin doing more of them. If he is not reading his Bible enough, instead of worrying about it, let him start reading it more. If he is not praying enough, the best solution is to pray more. And so on down the line.

But very often people who are so troubled will not find relief by increasing their performance and stepping up the quantity of prayers turned out or chapters read. Very likely they will be whipping up jaded nerves already exhausted, and will merely increase their load. After all, our Lord, when he invited us to take his yoke upon us and learn of him, went right on to add that his yoke was easy and his burden light. His commandments are not grievous. We should acquaint ourselves with God and be at peace, not perplexed.

What makes the trust of a child such a precious thing is that it does not go around all day wondering whether or not it is trusting its parents; wondering whether they will provide; wondering whether they love it; wondering whether their care will hold out. What a lot of things a child could worry about if it were like some Christians! And what a lot of things Christians would not worry about if they were childlike!

The fact is, the child does not think very often, if at all, about all these possible worries. And we prove our faith in God best by not talking so much about it, analyzing it, examining it. And we shall be healthier if we don't stick too many pins in ourselves. Let us have a good soul check-up now and then, see that everything is in order, then get busy for God; and most of our spiritual aches and pains will die of neglect.

Sometimes we need a spiritual operation: "If thy right hand offend thee, cut it off." Very well, let us have it and be done with it. Sometimes we need only to get out into God's sunshine. Sometimes, like Elijah, we need to feed and sleep. Sometimes we need simply to quit something we are doing or start something we are not doing. But whatever it is, let us do it and save for God the time we waste worrying because we are doing this or because we aren't doing that.

A little homely, sensible action, a simple taking ourselves by the back of the neck and making ourselves do what we ought to do will cure this God-dishonoring wallowing in the luxury of silly introspection. Stir up the gift of God within you, for God has not given us the spirit of fear but of power and of love and of a sound mind.

Chapter 12

Way Down in Tennessee

I'M way down South in a little place called South Pittsburg, Tennessee. Every little while in the course of my meanderings I strike a place this size and it always turns out to be a providential provision. I always seem to reach it just in time. I've been going pretty hard, and the Lord knew I'd need to come to a restful spot just about now.

I'm preaching in a little stone church, where we got off to a good start last night. This morning I've been strolling all over the little town, down shady streets and now and then out into the woods. It is late April and the tender green will never be this pretty again this year. There was a wood thrush singing on a hillside, and the vireos are carrying on their conversation in the treetops. The mockingbirds are in good practice by now, and the cardinals add color and music to the scene. This is my kind of country, just like where I grew up, and I like it. Next week I'll be going up to New York and Boston to preach. There are good folks up there and it is mighty nice of them to invite me, but a place like this seems just about my size.

After all, the really important things of life can be counted on your fingers and you can have them here as well, and maybe a little better, than in the crowded metropolis. To a discerning heart, life's necessities tend to grow simpler as he goes along. He learns to lighten his load and drop his excess baggage. He may start out craving caviar, but he will end up enjoying cabbage. Plainer things suffice.

Here you can have health, more of it indeed, for there are sunshine and air and the woods. Here you can have friends and time enough to talk to them. I was awakened this morning by people joking with each other in a good-natured give-and-take as they went to work. There is time to get acquainted. Maybe we learn too much about each other here, for they say, you can't see much in a little place, but what you hear makes up for it. But, anyhow, you don't lose the individual in the crowd.

And God is just as near. His peace and joy and life eternal are just as available here as anywhere. There is time to think upon him, to be still and know that he is God. I don't wonder that Jesus loved Bethany. It must have been a little place like this. He could get outdoors, and there was plenty of time, and there were friends, Mary and Martha and Lazarus. And just here is an angle of our Lord's earthly life that has always charmed me. Paul was the greatest New Testament character next to our Savior, but he was a city man. There is very little of the touch of nature and solitude in Paul. He was a busy, driving, restless soul, and I'm afraid I would soon have run out of breath trying to keep up with him. But one never gets that impression from Jesus. He worked in the city too, but he usually got away to the mountain, to the lake, to Bethany. He always balanced everything. The city man and the countryman can meet in Jesus. With all his labors, there were always calm and repose. He knew how to leave it all and come apart to rest a while. He could turn loose and let go. It is awfully hard for some of us to learn that.

Blessed is the man who knows how to divide his time between Jerusalem and Bethany, the metropolis and the mountain, the wrangling mart and the dusty lane.

CHAPTER 13

Figures Can Lie

ONE of the many delusions from which the minis-try needs to be delivered today is the notion that a preacher may be judged by the size of his crowd. There are some prophets in every generation who are called and gifted for leading the multitude and attracting the throng. More power to them. But straightway we get out on a limb and conclude that every brother who is not speaking to packed houses is a failure and that something is wrong with him.

Something may be wrong with him, and he should check up on himself, search his heart, and take stock. But if he finds nothing after an honest inventory, then he need not get under the juniper because he is not preaching to over-flow audiences. Once in a while some successful preacher is held up and this lesson is drawn: "This man gets crowds because he preaches the gospel. If Christ is preached, the crowd will still come, for he will draw all men unto himself." Thus the inference prevails that an unfilled house means unfaithful preaching.

Such argument is a lot of hocus-pocus. For one thing, some men who are not preaching the gospel are having crowds for, having itching ears, men are heaping to them-selves teachers; and the Athenians turn out for their kind. Then again, there are true and faithful pastors ministering to small flocks who are as consecrated to God, and some-times more so, than some of the headliners. It is true that

Christ draws; but men resist his drawing, and they resist the gospel and going to church.

Concerning the true preacher Alexander Whyte wrote:

> He may have, he usually has, but few people, as people go in our day, and the better the preacher, sometimes, the smaller the flock. It was so in our Master's case. The multitude followed after the loaves, but they fled from the feeding doctrines till he first tasted that dejection and that sense of defeat which so many of his best servants are fed on in this world. Still, as our Lord did not tune his pulpit to the taste of the loungers of Galilee, no more will a minister worth the name do anything else but press deeper and deeper into the depths of truth and life, till, as was the case with his Master, his followers, though few, will be all the more worth having.

Matthew Henry lamented over the poor response to his ministry and felt that his labors in his parish were done, since many had left and few had been added. But he still feeds us with messages not too well appreciated in his own time.

This worship of crowds is part of our Americanism, and a poor part. We are such confirmed lovers of big statistics, quantity production, and mass movement that we low-rate anything that does not run into big figures. The great god Ballyhoo has most of us on our faces, and any Hebrew children that will not prostrate themselves before him land in a fiery furnace. But in that furnace there is a fourth party "like the Son of God."

The Son of God trod this road. He had crowds at the beginning; but the closer he came to the cross, the thinner his crowd. And the closer we come to the cross and all it means, the fewer the people—but the better they are!

All of this can be twisted into an excuse for laziness on the part of some preachers who will not work. They are a different sort and must give account. But if a man be honest, right with God and men, and faithful, let him watch for souls and not for statistics. God keeps the books.

CHAPTER 14

Home Again

AFTER a year of preaching over the land I'm home again, back in the hills where I grew up. It has been a busy year of constant travel under the abnormal conditions of war. Of course, you can't get away from it all, even here, for three boys from this house are already in the service and another may go any day. But it is good to be still and catch my breath on the old hilltop, to sit under the oaks and look across the fields to the far-off skyline, to listen to the wood thrush sing morning and evening, as of yore. I like to return about once a year and have a little prayer meeting of my own out in the old familiar woods—to renew the covenant, as it were, and go back to Bethel. It renews my strength in more ways than one to get back to the source—back to the house where I was born, the hills I love, the woods where were dreamed the long, long dreams of youth; and then, better still, back to The Source, the one in whom we live and move and have our being.

I am resolved to escape now and then to the hills. We Christians have allowed this crazy age to steal from us the quiet hour. We too have been caught in the whirl, and we cannot minister to others because we are as tired and fever-ish and hurried as the world. It takes a real exercise of will to break out of the vicious circle, to take time and make time to come apart and rest a while. The whole setup of the age is against it.

This morning I hunted up my old walking stick. I am sure it has grown impatient, standing in a corner waiting for my return. I can imagine it complaining, "Dear me, he used to take me for a stroll every day, and then it was months and now it is a year from one ramble in the woods to another!" Nothing inanimate comes nearer taking on personality than a long-used walking stick. We set off down through the pasture and into the woods and followed the familiar water course around our favorite circle. We lay in the leaves and watched the clouds drift lazily by. Once more the ovenbird preached and the yellow-breasted chat went through his comic skit. There was even a blue grosbeak comfortably warbling on our way home.

The only break in our reverie was a pesky crow who found us and then kept broadcasting the whereabouts of the suspicious-looking newcomers. I was reminded of the fowls that broke in on Abraham's offering. The crow is one of nature's strange nuisances. In color, in habits, and especially by reason of his miserable cawing, he is a discordant note on any lovely day. What to do with him I do not know, except to grin and bear him. He is a fitting symbol of many other intrusions into our lives that do not appear to make much sense. There is no use bothering to explain these things; we accept them and remember that just because we cannot explain them does not mean that they cannot be explained.

I have just had word of the death of a preacher friend of mine, just about my own age. He passed away suddenly, in the midst of a fruitful ministry. I have been looking at a picture of him and myself with another minister whose life was suddenly snuffed out a few years ago in an automobile collision, a crash with a car driven by a drunken driver. Both of them taken out of fine and promising ministries—and now the survivor of this trio wonders why he has been permitted to remain. And why are so many useful souls taken and useless cumberers of the earth left? We know not, but, after all, that is God's business; and we will not use earth's fleeting time to unravel what only eternity can reveal.

CHAPTER 15

"Afar Off"

I'VE been down at my old home in the hills, and I've spent a lot of time on the front porch looking eastward across fields and woods to the far horizon, or perched on a rock looking westward across the hills to the mountain skyline. It is a great place to see "afar off."

Now I'm at Blowing Rock, high up in the mountains, much higher than my home, so I can see farther off than ever. Which sets me thinking about seeing afar off in a realm more wonderful than our eyes can behold.

It was Isaiah who wrote, "Thine eyes shall see the king in his beauty: they shall behold the land that is very far off." The fair King and the far country! When we really see the King by faith, what vistas open to the soul! There is the far country of the Christian life. Old things pass away and all things become new. We enter a different world; we become citizens of heaven. And no man has ever explored all the ranges of the life in Christ; there always remains much more land to be possessed.

There is the far country of service in the name of the King. Not that we have to go as missionaries to a foreign land, though it may mean that. Our far country may be across the street, not across the sea. And yet, right in the neighborhood where we live, there are unexplored worlds of service and testimony for us as ambassadors of Christ. One word spoken to a lone country boy may resound around the earth. Think of what a far country opened up when that humble Christian spoke to Dwight L. Moody in a shoe store!

And there is the far country of the life beyond, boundless, endless. Surely a saving look at the fair King opens up panoramas that no eye can compass. Eye nor ear nor heart can take in what God has prepared, but he has revealed them to us by his Spirit.

But some of us are cross-eyed and some are shortsighted, and we need to anoint our eyes with eye salve that we may see. Peter tells us that there are those who "cannot see afar off." Such Christians do not lay hold of the promises, they do not develop the Christian graces, they are not abounding Christians. Some of them are so busy looking at things near by that they miss the wide vision before them. Once I chanced upon a girl sitting on the rim of the Grand Canyon reading a novel! And how many miss the far view of the things of God and the world of the Spirit because they are taken up with the cheap little novel of themselves.

I have read of a city dweller whose eyes were giving him trouble. The doctor advised him to go to the mountains where he could see long distances. He had been penned up in city walls and needed the far look. Some of the saints need to get away like that.

In Hebrews we read of those heroes of faith who, "not having received the promises but having seen them afar off," were persuaded of them and embraced them and confessed that they were pilgrims and strangers on the earth. Abraham was one of these. He did not know where he was going immediately, but he knew where he was going ultimately. He did not know the whither but he knew the whom. He believed God; and, being sure of his destiny, he did not worry about his destination.

Let us see the fair King first, and then "anywhere with Jesus we can safely go." Like Paul, we follow the "who art thou, Lord?" with "Lord, what wilt thou have me to do?" We look up and then we look out, but not down. Elisha's servant looked the wrong way and saw only the adversary. When God opened his eyes he saw horses and chariots of fire. The prayer of his master befits many of us shortsighted saints today—"Lord, open his eyes, that he may see."

CHAPTER 16

Wells

IS there anything that entangles itself more in our memories than the old well back home? While I was there on my all-too-short visit this summer, I recaptured a little of the knack of drawing water without spilling it. Each morning I went out on the back porch, pitcher in hand, and let the old bucket down swiftly, putting brakes on the windlass as soon as the bucket struck the water. There is an art, you know, in not unwinding too much rope for, like so many things in life, what you unwind easily must be wound up again laboriously. Then the upward pull; and, although many years have passed since I was the official drawer of water (as well as hewer of wood), I found myself instinctively slowing up just when the bucket reached the curb.

I do not wonder that old wells and old oaken buckets have endeared themselves in human hearts through the ages. I can understand David's wanting a drink of water from the well at Bethlehem. In the storm and stress of life our hearts turn back to the old, satisfying things; and a drink from the old well means more than any concoctions this present day can mix. Dr. Torrey tells how, when he was in China and for some days in a disease-infected spot, they were allowed to have only bottled drinks, his thoughts turned back to the old well in New England. What he would have given for a cool, sparkling draught from home!

The Bible is full of wells, experiences around wells, wells as figures of spiritual satisfaction. Abraham dug wells, the

Philistines filled them up, and Isaac had to dig them out again. Our fathers dug spiritual wells in this country and we have let the Philistines fill them. We have allowed the same thing in our own lives, and we must clear out the sticks and stones and dirt and debris. There is no use asking God to do it. Isaac didn't ask the Lord to send down angels with picks and shovels; he dug out the wells. The water will rise if the well is cleaned out. There is no point in asking the Lord to fill us with the Spirit if we are already filled with something else.

The well that comes most readily to mind is Jacob's well, with Jesus and the Samaritan woman. She asked, "Art thou greater than our father Jacob which gave us this well?" Men today are doubting anything better than Jacob and his wells – the natural, the ordinary, the material. Millions do not think there is any better satisfaction than Jacob and his well can supply. So they forsake the fountain of living waters and hew them out cisterns, broken cisterns that can hold no water.

But Jesus is greater than Jacob. Men keep coming back to Jacob's well. That is exactly what Jesus said to the woman: "Whosoever drinketh of this water shall thirst again: but whosoever drinketh of the water that I shall give him shall never thirst: but the water that I shall give him shall be in him a well of water springing up into everlasting life." Now, here is a blessed thing often overlooked. I hear Christians bemoaning their spiritual dissatisfaction. They are still thirsting. Of course, there is always more to learn; we are to grow and increase and press on. But we are not to run back every little while for a fresh drink and then keep going until that gives out. Jesus expressly said, "shall never thirst again." And more than that, this living water becomes a well within us! Why should we be running back for a drink if we have a well in ourselves? The point is, we are so to abide in him that we are not empty pitchers to be filled but fountains with the channel clear and the stream ever flowing. He also said that from within us should flow rivers of living water. Of course, if the channel is clogged we have a duty to clean it out and remove the hindrance. Some mistakenly ask for more water: take away the obstruction and the water will flow! We are to "drink and keep on drinking"; it is a life of constant receiving and constant overflowing.

CHAPTER 17

Sharpening the Axe

ONE of the many memories that comes drifting back to me from boyhood days in the hills is of that occasional ordeal, sharpening the axe. Every little while—far too often, I thought—father would arrive at the fixed and unalterable conclusion that it was time to give the old axe a going over. I can conceive of no operation more monotonous, tiresome, and unromantic. It was a grind in more ways than one. Hoeing corn was hard work, but there was at least the advantage of moving from place to place; and there was always the possibility that a bird's nest might turn up somewhere to relieve the tedium.

But sharpening the axe! Father always held the axe and I turned the grindstone. Anybody could turn the grindstone, but it took ability and judgment to hold the axe just right for the final desired effect, an edge neither too thin nor too dull. What a welcome moment when father for the umpteenth time flicked the edge with his finger, appraised it with squinted eye, and declared it just right. And it had to be just right! Long after I would have declared that it would split hairs we toiled until father's exacting requirements were fully met.

The years have passed: father and the axe and the grindstone have gone, but the turner of the grindstone remains. And to him since then have come precious lessons from the homely things of long ago. Life is simply the repetition in different spheres and on a different scale of the humble exercises of youth. How many axes need to be sharpened in the course of the years!

The Old Testament account of the lost axe-head in the ministry of Elisha has often been the basis of messages on lost spiritual power. It is a good application. But the axe-head may not be lost and yet it may be dull. And next to a lost axe-head the worst thing possible is a dull axe-head. The spiritual edge of our lives may be blunted, and as a consequence the chopping will be laborious and the chips few.

It has been said, "He who waits on God loses no time." He who takes time out to sharpen his spiritual axe-head is wise. Somewhere we have read of a wood-chopper whose chips were few. Somebody reminded him that his axe-head was dull and should be sharpened. "Indeed, I won't stop for that," he answered; "I am far behind now with my chopping, and if I take time out to sharpen the axe I will never catch up." It is ridiculous but often true in the things of the Spirit. How many Christians are too busy, even with good things, to have a time of renewing, time to take stock and wait on the Lord! How many churches are too occupied with their programs to have a revival! The routine must be kept up in the strength of the flesh if not in the Spirit. It never seems to occur to them that more wood could be chopped in less time if the axe were sharpened.

Perhaps we do not sharpen the axe because it means work and hard, unromantic effort. Our lives need a going over now and then and the flesh does not relish it. There are nicks and gaps in our souls that need to be ground out on the grindstone of repentance and prayer, but we rebel. We must take ourselves seriously in hand if our spirits are to be kept on edge. The steady application of the means of grace is tedious to the old nature. We must diligently hold the axe and turn the grindstone.

But if we thus study to show ourselves approved unto God, there will be compensation in being workmen who need not be ashamed, rightly dividing the Word of Truth. Nothing worthwhile comes easily. The tedious axe-grinding of boyhood days has been duplicated again and again in other realms and still the old lesson remains: It pays to take time to sharpen the axe!

CHAPTER 18

Memories

SOME little recollections that filter down through the years: rhubarb pie back home, the "stickies" that mother used to make with left-over dough when the biscuits were all made—better than any sweet roll I've tried since. And those lucky days when I was allowed to scrape out the cake batter left in the bowl.

The corn shucking when it had rained all week and all our pies had spoiled. Coming home in the old surrey from night meeting at Corinth Church—and how sleepy! Wheat-threshing time and my boyish fear of steam engines. The time I ate all the bananas in father's store and didn't die. The old soda-water bottles that were plugged inside and were opened by banging in the plug.

Grandma and her visits. Her square, old-timey suitcase and her bottle of magic oil that cured just about everything. Grandpa and his animal books that always took up the whole afternoon when I went to his house. The old honeysuckle vine on the back porch and how I used to pull out the pistil to find the drop of honey. Saturday night before the fourth Sunday when the preacher always stayed at our house. Going out to Uncle Peter's to hear him play the talking machine. Swinging under the big oak in the back yard and wishing I could fly.

The old lamps on the wall at Corinth Church and how one was almost always smoking during the sermon, with its wick turned up far too high. The book we used to have, *Sermons By The Devil:* how I shuddered at the picture of the death of a bad man with devils all around him, and felt better when the next page showed a dying Christian with angels coming to carry him home.

I wonder if anybody still makes green huckleberry pie. The spelling match at the schoolhouse on Friday afternoons. Father's derby—for years he never wore any other kind of hat. The "blouse" I wore with a puckering-string at the bottom. Our talking-machine with the cylinder records. That bitter medicine I used to take for "the catarrh." My first ride in a Ford, holding on to my cap and going every bit of twenty-five miles an hour. My uncle's Buick with the right-hand drive, no doors in front. The dusters we wore on those early auto adventures over dirt roads.

Good old days when we had time to think. Countrified ways and hillbilly manners but hearts of gold. Of course, I know that not everybody can grow up in the sticks; some people must suffer the disadvantages of town, but I don't hold it against them; they can't help it. The only difference between city folks and country folks is, the city folks came to the city from the country and couldn't get back. One thing I do know: You can pick up town ways later on, but if you didn't grow up in the country, you can't learn country ways. You can wear overalls and a straw hat and try to look rustic but it "ain't natural," and there's all the difference that there is between a dude rancher and a real cowboy. You can't learn it; you have to be born and grow up that way.

Which applies to other things more profound. Joining a church or being the husband of a good wife doesn't make a man a citizen of heaven's kingdom either. It isn't earned or learned nor entered by naturalization papers. You have to be born and grow up there.

CHAPTER 19

Old Shep

IT was a cynic who said, "The more I see of people, the better I like my dog." I would not wish to be so bitter about humanity, but I did think a lot of my dog.

Old Shep grew up with me on the little farm back home. He had no aristocratic ancestors and won no blue ribbons at dog shows. He was just plain dog. He was my constant companion and bodyguard. When an uncle from out West came to visit us, he picked me up and I started to cry; in a flash Shep leaped upon the uncle's back and would have done plenty of damage had not Father come to the rescue.

Boy and dog, we roamed the woods together. For sheer human delight, I wonder if I have ever been happier than when I started out some May morning from that little Carolina hilltop, while yellow-hammers and cardinals and wood thrushes staged their gayest concert, while the bees worked the blossoms and butterflies did their elfin dance through the orchard—started out with Shep, just rambling. I never knew a morning when he was not as keen to start as I. I don't think he ever quite understood why I just looked at birds and never hunted them. Sometimes he shook his head despairingly when I missed good chances to catch or shoot those elusive warblers and sparrows. I am sure that he never shared my ideas about ornithology; with him a bird in the mouth was worth two in the bush. But if he never tasted bird meat for all his woodland jaunts, there

67

were other compensations; and he seemed happy just to be with me. And when we trudged home at midday for dinner (not lunch—that word is too weak for what I could eat at noon those days), no millionaire in fancy togs at some high-priced resort could buy the joy that we had free of charge those bright May mornings.

What fools we mortals be! We build our pleasure palaces and spend our savings chasing from the sea to the mountains and from the mountains to the sea, and all the while a country boy with a dog has more fun in a minute than all the vacationists.

My mind can reconstruct today some of the trails that Shep and I used to take. Past the old apple tree and the bee-hives (once in a while Shep had an unfortunate experience when a bee got tangled in his woolly mane; he had even less enthusiasm for beekeeping than for bird study); then down through the nearby woods, past the big dogwood bush and through the honeysuckle; next there was a little ravine, then a neighbor's cabin and a busy brook—a "branch" in those days—and, just beyond that, deeper woods into which we dared not go. Africa was scarcely more remote than the depths of those dark woods. Occasionally Shep and I looked wistfully into those wilds and half resolved to explore them; but discretion prevailed and we contented ourselves within reach of home. There was plenty to investigate within our range: birds' nests and huckleberries and strange flowers and always big stones to overturn, to the consternation of creeping things beneath; crawfish in the "branch"; and, once in a while, a rabbit would leap out before us to tantalize Shep to a fruitless chase.

Simple things! Ah, yes, but precious things that linger after many later issues we thought "momentous" have been forgotten. And methinks that in the world of spirit too we spin many mysteries and fret our souls over theological conundrums, when the simple things are most abiding. Did he not say, "Except ye be converted and become as little children..."?

Shep grew old, and one day we buried him down in "the hollow." I was growing up and newer interests claimed my attention. But here I am thinking of Shep again and am quite convinced that much which has glittered since his day was not gold. The Bible tells us that without the gates of the heavenly city are dogs. It does not mean the four-legged kind, of course; but doubtless more than one saint, though he would never admit it in prayer meeting, has secretly wished that within might be his dog. I do know that the Word holds hope of animals at peace in the millennium, so perhaps it is not heresy to envision a stroll with a companionable dog as a bit of millennial bliss.

CHAPTER 20

An "Inside" Vacation

A wise bit of medical advice in a recent newspaper column recommends learning to relax all along instead of living in a fever for months and then trying to make up for it with a vacation.

It is sensible counsel. Nature never intended that we should drive ourselves to the breaking point, then try to regain in a month what we spent in a year. She would have us live relaxed lives all along or at least catch our breath for a spell daily instead of running up a physical debt which we have not time to pay.

In other words, we should learn to take an "inside" vacation, within ourselves. Merely taking an "outside" vacation, changing the scenery, will do no good if the same old inner strain goes along. "Getting away from it all" is usually a great delusion, for we generally take it all with us.

And yet we can learn to get away from it all right in the midst of it all. I recall a word which a friend of mine who had gone through great trouble dropped in a conversation. "When I go to bed at night," he said, "I just close the door on it all." Of course, other people have said that, but my friend really did it; he simply bolted the door of his mind on all his fears and worries instead of taking them to bed with him. And why not? They will be no worse tomorrow for having been dismissed for the night, and he will certainly be all the stronger and better when morning comes.

To be sure, it is well and good to escape to the mountains or the shore if you can. But not everybody can, and far better it is to live daily, resting on the inside. It can be done. Simple faith in God through Christ, obedience to his will, the Bible, prayer, a sense of humor, and good common sense can save us from collapses; and by daily renewing our strength we can mount up with wings as eagles, run and not be weary, walk and not faint.

Make sure of your salvation and live in the will of God. Learn to live calmly a day at a time. It is not learned in a day, but every day you practice it you are taking the best medicine in the world. "A merry heart doeth good like a medicine," and the cultivation of a serene spirit is worth all the vacations. It is not work but worry that kills, and it is amazing how much wear the human mind and body can stand if it is free from friction and well oiled by the Spirit. A mind at leisure from itself beats all the rest cures.

Taking a vacation on the inside, within one's own self, is not popular, for it calls for a denial and a dedication and a discipline which most folk do not care to make. So they take the other kind and rush around all cluttered up with their toggery without and their troubles within.

Jesus gave us the secret long ago: "Come unto me, all ye that labor and are heavy laden, and I will give you rest." Then he added, "Take my yoke upon you and learn of me; for I am meek and lowly in heart: and ye shall find rest unto your souls." His rest is both obtained and attained. It is ours in Christ, but we realize it daily as we follow him. And he said, "My yoke is easy and my burden is light." There is rest in the very practice of his will, for we are free from the friction of care and fear. His rest is not for loafers but for learners; but as we learn, we are lightened. It is a foretaste of heaven, where we ever serve the King but never grow tired at all.

CHAPTER 21

Snubbing "The Sticks"

THEORETICALLY, we claim to believe that the country and country folks are the backbone of the nation, but actually we don't live up to that belief. It is a compliment we pay the ruralites at picnics or when running for office, but most of us desert the country quickly enough when the town beckons.

As soon as the rising doctor, preacher, teacher, or businessman discovers that he has some ability, he casts his eyes toward the metropolis. Somehow, we have developed the absurd notion that the best in any profession end up in the city. Often that leaves the country people, the cream of the land, to get along with whatever they can get when they deserve the best.

By what reasoning process do you conclude that a country preacher should be regarded as inferior to a city minister? It is true that country preachers are very often young men just getting started or old men who have had their day, but it is ridiculous to infer that a preacher is "good" in the proportion to which he has been recognized on the boulevard. To be sure, there are good preachers in town. Anybody who can live in a modern city and stay good deserves honorable mention. But they do not exhaust the list of pulpit worthies. Some of the best preachers who ever lived are out in "the sticks," laboring with scanty means and plentiful adversities. It is no reflection upon them that no town has recognized their merits. Sometimes it is to their credit.

But, for all that, havoc is being wrought by this false standard of values. The country should have the best of everything. Too many rising stars snub the hills and fields for an urban opportunity and leave their greatest chance behind. If it were not for our clodhoppers the bottom would have fallen out of civilization long ago. The world has been held together by rustics who say "seen" for "saw" and who, perchance, still cool their coffee in the saucer. But deterioration has set in because the crazy doctrine that the best things are in town has infected the country. There was a time when rural youngsters could find enough to entertain them without driving into the burg for a licentious show.

The notion that no one has arrived until some town has endorsed him has ruined more than one career that was adapted to rural work but out of place on Main Street. There will be a shift of emphasis one of these days and we shall awake to see where our treasures lie. There is no better opportunity for any promising young man than to live and labor with the hayseeds. From our cornfields and potato patches our future leaders, if we ever have any, will come.

Many of the Bible's biggest preachers stayed in the "sticks." It will pay the spiritual descendants of Elijah, Amos, and John the Baptist to stay in the tall timber. And the greatest of all loved the hills and lakes of Galilee.

One of these days some preacher is going to see the point and settle down far from the madding crowd's ignoble strife to preach and work the rest of his days as though the country were not just a springboard from which to leap into town. I venture that the woods and fields will give his sermons a flavor no city office could bestow. And from his church strong young men and women will go forth to serve the King to the ends of the earth. And I think that towns and cities may one day invite this preacher to come over and tell them what he learned in the "sticks" while they were going to civic functions and dodging traffic and waiting for elevators and otherwise enjoying the benefits of progress.

CHAPTER 22

Shoppers and Soul-Winners

I am not concerned now with the main points usually brought out in the account of Jesus and the woman at Jacob's well but rather with some interesting side-lights. We read that the disciples were gone away into the city to buy meat. While they were gone Jesus talked with this woman. The disciples returned, and she went into the city and brought the Samaritans out to see Jesus. The disciples asked Jesus to eat, but he told them his meat was to do God's will.

It will be observed that it was not the disciples who went into Samaria and brought Samaritans out to see Jesus. One would have expected it to happen that way. Were they not his followers, the ones best qualified to witness for him? But they were in town merely to look for something to eat, and a brand-new convert did the soul-winning.

Again and again, we have discovered that it is not the ones we would have expected to do it who bring people to Jesus. The general run of disciples these days is not in Samaria witnessing. They are shopping, not soul-winning. On Sunday morning there are more whose thoughts at church turn at noon to the Sunday dinner rather than to the meat that perisheth not. The average Christian is out looking for meat and can move through a city seeing shops but not souls.

Here was a woman, a new recruit, with very little instruction, who did the work. Time and again, we have been shamed by the zeal of young Christians who went after Samaritans and got them while we merely shopped in Samaria, seeking our own, feeding our stomachs instead of our souls.

Our Lord told these disciples, "I have meat to eat that ye know not of. My meat is to do the will of him that sent me and finish his work." To do God's will is food, not fetters. We go about it as though it were a chore. It was Jesus' meat and drink.

Then he said, "Say not ye, There are yet four months and then cometh harvest? Behold, I say unto you, Lift up your eyes and look on the fields; for they are white already to harvest." We still talk that way. There is no urgency about it. We fold our hands and say, "Lord, save the sinners." He saved us to go after the sinners! Jesus prayed for us, not for the world, and he expects us to go seek the lost. The Bible says little about sinners going to church. It tells us to go, then get out and bring in the sinners. It has been said, "It would be a good thing if churches were closed one year and the people compelled to go out and serve instead of come in and sit." An overstatement, maybe, but there is a truth in it.

The shepherd went after the sheep. Nowadays we have built comfortable folds and have put on the outside: "Any lost sheep reporting here will be taken care of."

So, while we are shopping in Samaria, less privileged souls put us to shame with their soul-winning. I think of an old brother, with only one eye—and he has to hold a double magnifying glass sideways to read with that one— who studies his Bible, has a lot of good books, and goes after sinners, perhaps a bit bluntly sometimes, but at least he is not merely shopping in Samaria. It is not four months until harvest with him, it is harvest now; and he is out in the wheatfield up to his ears, while others, better gifted and educated, are discussing ways and means.

"He that reapeth receiveth wages and gathereth fruit unto life eternal." This is no time to be looking for meat for the body, merely shopping in Samaria. God give us some more fresh Christians who are busy inviting men to come see one "who told me all things that ever I did." These have meat that most of us know not of.

CHAPTER 23

The Law of Character

IT is an old, old adage that "thoughts produce acts, acts produce habits, and habits produce character." And it is a pity that we do not remember it better in our Christian living. We are so prone to expect to become good Christians by some sudden experience that lifts us all at once to higher ground without the gradual climb. We forget that we are to "grow in grace" and that normal growth is not a matter of fits and starts.

The laws of the spiritual world are not unpredictable affairs of caprice. They are orderly, and certain causes produce certain results. Our adage is a safe yardstick, and it begins with our thoughts. "As he thinketh in his heart so is he" has wider application among us than in the original verse. We are bidden to think on those things that will produce acts pleasing to God. A man can control his thoughts. He cannot help evil thoughts coming along, but he does not have to invite them to come in and make themselves at home. Our defeat or victory begins with what we think, and if we guard our thoughts we shall not have much trouble anywhere else along the line.

"Thoughts produce acts," and we should attend to it that our holy thoughts get expressed in holy deeds. Goethe said, "Thought without action is a disease," and there are many sick saints thus afflicted. Hearers of the Word but not doers, they deceive themselves; doctrine is never translated into

81

duty, creed never becomes deed. They never bring the vision down to the valley, and so they deteriorate into dreamers, emotional drunkards, rich as Solomon one day and down with a hangover the next. They revel in lofty ideas that never get hitched to practical service. So one has written:

> Think not the faith by which the just shall live
> Is a dead creed, a map correct of heaven;
> Far less a feeling, fond and fugitive.
> It is an affirmation and an act
> That bids eternal truth be present fact.

Indeed, it is "an affirmation and an act," and holy acts repeated enough become fixed habits. Right here so many saints miss the track. They disregard the law of habit, and because holy deeds seem unnatural the first few times they do them, they give them up before they become the fixed practice of their lives. Any practice seems unnatural at first. Learning to drive a car is awkward business, but persisted in long enough it becomes second nature. So the doing of God's will does not seem easy at first. Oh, I know that the love of God transforms drudgery into delight; but the mechanics of good deeds are not always pleasant, and we must keep doing the thing we ought to do until it becomes the "natural" thing and anything else seems "unnatural." Practice makes perfect, and no emotional experience or mountain-top vision will take the place of the law of habit.

Then, as we control our thoughts, translate thoughts into deeds, and steadily practice the deeds, we form character, the inevitable result. Take care of the first three steps and character will take care of itself. There is no need of pulling up the seed to see whether it is sprouting or by taking thought trying to add cubits to the stature.

To be sure, we read that as we behold the glory of the Lord we are changed into the same image. It is the work of the Holy Spirit. But we are not automatons; we have a will and a responsibility. We are responsible for what we do about our thoughts, acts, and habits. As we consent to obey God in all three, he works in us to will and do. The indwelling Christ reproduces himself in us as we trust and obey. A Christian character is the product in the life of him who thinks, does, and practices the will of God.

There is nothing hit or miss about it. "Think on these things." "If ye know these things, happy are ye if ye do them." Practice "patient continuance in well doing." Look into the perfect law of liberty and continue therein!

4 Bible verses right here!

Chapter 24

A Word to Prospective Maniacs

I am convinced that if the devil cannot make us lazy, he will make us so busy here and there that the best is sacrificed for the good. I once thought that every invitation I received as a speaker was the leading of the Lord. But I discovered that I was sometimes invited to speak at two different places at the same time, and I knew that the Lord knew I was singular, not plural. From that, I went on to learn that I had been given some common sense and was expected to use it under the Spirit's direction.

We display the Lord's leading as much by what we refuse as by what we accept. The Lord is not interested in mere quantity production. We can often do more by doing less. It is no mark of godliness to be forever running about in a fever, our tongues hanging out, in a glorified St. Vitus's dance. These dear souls who argue that the devil never takes a vacation should remember that we are not supposed to imitate the devil. We follow the Lord, who was unhurried and who said, "Come ye yourselves apart and rest awhile."

It is high time we learned that in this nerve-wrecking, maddening modern rush, we have let the spirit of the times rob us utterly of meditation, devotion, rest, the passive side of our Christian experience without which we cannot be truly active to the glory of God. There is no depth to us. We are all whizzing around from preacher to preacher, meeting to meeting, with pad and pencil, hiding the Word in our notebooks instead of in our hearts. A lot of our Christian life and work is frothy, superficial, thin. We are growing mushrooms, not oaks.

I have learned long since that when I arrive in a place and calls descend like locusts to come to this meeting, grab a sandwich and hop to another, address the Whoozits at ten and the Whatsits at eleven, only to arrive at the main meeting woozy and exhausted, that part of a preacher's best equipment is a good healthy No. It looks good, but it is a subtle snare; and both we and the good people who invite us are unwittingly deceived by it. If either we or they took second thought we could see that we defeat our own purposes when we spread ourselves too thinly, striking everywhere and hitting hard nowhere. We Christians often lead dissipated lives, squandering our energies in a multitude of good things but becoming so exhausted that none of it counts for much.

The temptation is great for an aggressive preacher to run a church, hold outside meetings, carry a radio program, put on a Bible school, edit a magazine, write books, and from there on add a new sideline every little while, until he ends up in a hospital. Once in a while there is a Hercules who can stand it, but is it the best way? The old saints did a few things well, as a rule. They took time to be still, and we go back to them now to feed our souls. They produced cream, and it takes time for cream to rise.

If our lives and ministry count for anything today, we must solemnly resolve to make time for God. It is not easy. Some people won't like it, but somebody else wouldn't like it if we did some other way, so that doesn't matter. We must make out a schedule and work out a program at all costs that will eliminate the nonessential (including a lot of things some dear souls will think are very essential), put first things first, and make a lot of second-rate things stay in line, no matter how much they clamor for first place.

It is the best way to get to heaven without detouring by an insane asylum. And you will make a life as well as a living, and stay not only clothed but in your right mind.

CHAPTER 25

Ministry in Old Rags

WE are familiar with the New Testament Ethiopian eunuch who was won to Christ by Philip as he read the prophecy of Isaiah. But there is an Old Testament Ethiopian eunuch who is not so well known as he should be.

Jeremiah had been cast into a dungeon and was in dire distress, sunk in the mire. Ebed-melech, the Ethiopian, one of the eunuchs in the king's house, went to Zedekiah and protested. The king sent him with thirty men to rescue the prophet. They went to the dungeon and let down cords with "old cast clouts and old rotten rags," and Ebed-melech instructed Jeremiah to put these rags under his armholes to protect his flesh while they pulled him up. God remembered this kindly deed and promised the eunuch his life in the evil day ahead.

Now I am intrigued by these old rotten rags. What an extra touch it adds to this story of a merciful servant rescuing a mighty prophet! Ebed-melech could have let down ropes and pulled up Jeremiah, rags or no rags. Jeremiah ought to be glad to get out of that dungeon even with raw and bleeding armpits. But Ebed-melech's goodness is the sort that does not forget details. And the Word of God takes up space to tell us about a ministry in cast-off clouts and old rotten rags.

Blessed are those saints who belong to the order of Ebed-melech. They never preach great sermons nor do they

89

crash the headlines with some astounding feat of godliness. But they are the unsung heroes of the cup of cold water in Jesus' name. They make the bed smoother for some weary invalid; they cook some tired preacher an appetizing meal; they leave a bushel of potatoes at some back door and drive off without waiting for thanks; they sit up some long, lonely night with some distressed soul who cannot sleep. They were never meant to be teachers, prophets, or evangelists; but they are "helps," and they are the sort who when a relief expedition is being organized think about the old rags to protect the prophet's armpits. Their greatness consists in doing nobly a multitude of unromantic things.

I once heard a preacher say: "I used to load my gun with powder and shot and wadding when I went hunting. I never killed anything with the wadding, but, then, I never killed anything without the wadding. If you can't be powder and shot for God, you can wad!" Which was another way of saying that you can think of the old rags to make the prophet's deliverance a little less painful!

So here is a way to be a ragman for God. Not all the rewards of heaven will go to the great preachers. There will be a special prize, for instance, for godly church janitors who couldn't preach but who could make it a sight easier for somebody to preach who could. Our Lord commended the woman who anointed him with costly ointment, but here God commends a friend who offered only rags! Whether rags or riches, nothing escapes him who sits by heaven's treasury and sees what we give. Whether mite or much, it is the spirit that glorifies the gift.

If you cannot be a Jeremiah, you can be an Ebed-melech. A black man carried the Savior's cross in the New Testament. And in the Old, a black man rescued a sinking prophet. What a roll heaven will reveal of lowly folks who have had a share in the program of God! How blessed to know that the Almighty, with a whole universe on his hands, caught a glimpse of Ebed-melech with those old rotten rags, preserved him from judgment, and remembered his rags in the holy record. If one man got into the Bible with a handful of rags, think not that your service will pass unseen. If it come from a heart that loves him, it will not escape his kindly notice.

A ministry in rags! Blessed be the order of Ebed-melech!

Chapter 26

Only a Step

"There is but a step between me and death" (1 Sam. 20:3).

SO spake David to Jonathan. And so may we all say. For death is not something away out yonder somewhere, it is all about us, close at hand.

I have looked out from the window of a high building and have reflected that only a few inches lie between me and the world to come. Riding on the train, it has occurred to me that if those wheels went a few inches to the right or left, I might embark into the beyond. In your medicine cabinet there is perhaps a bottle of poison, and every time you open the door you are just that close to death. In fact, it advertises itself with skull and crossbones on the label. Every day, in a multitude of ways, you could take one step and be gone. There is but a step between us and death.

In the midst of life we are in the midst of death. Think not of it as a remote possibility; it is a present actuality, right here and now. And if death is so close, so are heaven and hell. One minute and we can be out of time and into eternity. Too long have we fancied the future state as a dim, far-off realm, and have forgotten how quickly we can be there. One may feel that way about China, for, with all our modern travel, China is still a good way off. But you do not go to heaven or hell as you go to China. It is only a step.

If it is only a step to heaven, it is only a step to God. Think not of him as a distant deity far removed from all our ups and downs. He is in heaven, but he is also wherever a seeking soul would search for him with all the heart. It is only a step to Jesus for the Christian. Wherever we gather in his name, he is there. He is, indeed, nearer than breathing, closer than hands or feet. And for the sinner it is only a step to salvation. One minute he may be under condemnation, lost and undone; the next, rejoicing in a Savior's love.

And while we make our way through this world and sometimes are almost overwhelmed by the things of sense and sight, let us not forget that all about us is a world unseen and that we can enter it whenever we will by the step of prayer. John G. Paton's father had a little corner of his home curtained off to which he often repaired to have a word with God. It was only a step out of the seen into the unseen. I have read of a poor tenement mother whose living quarters were so crowded that she could secure privacy only by throwing her apron over her head as now and then she had a word with heaven. It was a hard expedient, but she had learned that only a step could put her in touch with the eternal.

Those who know how to take only a step and be with God do indeed "ply their daily task with busier feet because their secret souls a holier strain repeat." Theirs is the closet of prayer, and while "one listening even cannot know when they have crossed the threshold o'er, he who knows and understands has heard the shutting of the door." What a difference one short hour spent in his presence can make!

What a shame, then, that at any time it is only a step within the veil and we blunder along so miserably without it! A shop worker had over her machine a sign, "When the Threads Get Tangled, Call for the Foreman." One day the threads were all mixed up and she tried to untangle them with the result that they were tangled all the more.

The foreman came along, saw her predicament, and asked, "Didn't you see the sign?" "Yes," she sighed, "but I was doing my best to untangle them myself." "Madam," he replied, "doing your best is sending for the foreman!"

If the threads are tangled, call on the Foreman. It is only a step into his presence.

good!

CHAPTER 27

Who Is "Cultured"?

IT is high time that we had a fresh examination of that word "culture." Too long has culture meant college degrees, ability to talk about art and literature, several trips abroad, and proficiency in etiquette. Now, all these things are perfectly desirable and profitable, but they do not constitute culture. Two of the most highly literate nations of the world have lately plunged it into an agony of blood and tears. And plenty of individuals who have all the assets listed above are grand rascals and crooks supreme.

Long, long ago an old book set forth a different standard of culture: "He that ruleth his spirit [is better] than he that taketh a city" (Prov. 16:32). Now, we still glory in taking cities, the spectacular, the sensational thing. It makes the headlines. It summons the news reporters. It gets into the news reels. But God rates highest the man who rules his spirit. Here is a different aristocracy.

The really cultured person is the person with a cultivated soul. "The soul of progress is the progress of the soul." God would have us prosper only as our souls prosper (3 John 2). There are plain, poor people who cross our paths to shame us along this line. They have none of our proud marks of culture but they are cultured. I know a Negro elevator girl who has more culture than most of the mortals she hauls up and down in that hotel. They would be insulted if I told them so, but their culture won't begin to compare with hers. Some of them are very smart and can talk glibly about subjects supposed to require intelligence, but they are not cultured. Their souls are measly and undernourished, and some of them are vicious and evil-tempered and selfish and sour. They may talk some of the language of the cultured, but they are ignorant and coarse in their souls. But the elevator girl has the spirit of culture. Her heart is right and her manner declares a deeper loveliness than education, money, or travel can ever bestow.

But I do not speak of mere self-control. Some rule themselves with an iron will, live very decently, make themselves shun the wrong and do the right; but that is not culture. When Jesus was on earth, his bitterest enemies were religious folk who thought themselves very cultured spiritually. They knew the Scriptures, were steeped in tradition, kept a strict code of morals, prayed in public, gave a tenth of their income to God, and were so rigorously correct that they would not even eat an egg that had been laid on the Sabbath. But their spirits were all wrong. They thought they saw but were blind. Then Jesus came with a different sort of culture. And he reminded his hearers that unless their righteousness exceeded that of these scribes and Pharisees, they could not enter into the kingdom of heaven.

The truly cultured are those who have come to Jesus for salvation and are following him. He lives in their hearts, and as they yield to and obey him, his Spirit controls them, and they become daily more like him. The Holy Spirit produces in them love, joy, peace, long-suffering, gentleness, goodness, faith, meekness, temperance, which are the marks of culture.

You will notice that there is nothing very sensational about these graces. They do not make the headlines. There is a whole chapter in First Corinthians that describes the marks of love, and, strangely enough, the very things that do make the headlines, eloquence, wisdom, benevolence, martyrdom, are quickly discounted. But there is a higher aristocracy of the spirit and a deeper culture of soul. Let us seek them above all else.

CHAPTER 28

To Know and Not to Know

"It is given unto you to know" (Matt. 13:11).

"It is not for you to know." (Acts 1:7).

SOME things are for us to know, some things are not for us to know. Blessed is the man who learns early which is which. Most of our unhappiness is caused by not knowing what we should know and by trying to know what we are not to know.

The supreme privilege of life is to know Christ. That was Paul's motto: "To know him." Of course, he already knew Christ as Savior and had so known him ever since the day of the Damascus Road. But there is a gradual knowledge: "Then shall we know as we follow on to know the Lord." We are to grow in grace and in the knowledge of Christ. Too often we think of the Christian life in terms of rules and doctrines and church activities and forget that it is a personal faith in and fellowship with the living Christ. We can know a lot about Christ and do a lot for Christ and not know him.

But, of course, there is much to know about him too. We are witnesses unto him and witnesses "of these things," the truths concerning him. He invites us to come to him and receive rest, learn of him and find rest. In him are hid all the treasures of wisdom and knowledge and he is made unto us wisdom.

It is our privilege to know him personally, to know the truths concerning him and also the truths he taught. He was speaking of that in the verse with which we started. I am afraid that some of us have greatly neglected the Christ of the Gospels these days. Some have dwelt entirely on his teachings before the cross as though he were only a teacher of a way of life. Others, emphasizing that the gospel message is Christ dead and risen, have almost ignored the days of his flesh before Calvary. But we who believe in him are to walk as he walked, and to know how he walked we need to walk with him in the Gospels. There is not one word of his teachings that does not have a very pertinent message for us today.

Blessed is the man who learns what is given to him to know. We err because we know not the Scriptures or the power of God. Most of our misery is due to ignorance, and often wilful ignorance. But there is much trouble due to trying to know what we are not to know. The disciples wanted to know if Jesus would restore the kingdom to Israel. Now we believe that there will be a literal kingdom, but too many dear souls wear themselves out trying to figure out the mysteries of prophecies when they might be witnessing here and now to a living Christ.

And there are many other things we bother about which we are not to know. Peter wanted to know what would happen to John. We are always wondering what is going to become of this man and that movement. We need our Lord's rejoinder, "What is that to thee? Follow thou me."

Then we bother a lot about happenings in our own lives which we cannot understand. Job and Habakkuk tried to understand why they had so much trouble. They were not given explanation but revelation; they saw the Lord. Which brings us back to our starting point. The best way to be cured of worrying about what we are not to know is to get better acquainted with what we are to know, with him whom we should know.

Like it! 9/21/19
Sat. night !

CHAPTER 29

The Revivalist Who Backslid

IT was an evil time in Bethel. Jeroboam brazenly offered incense at the altar. God raised up a prophet to pronounce judgment in the very presence of the king. And when Jeroboam tried to lay hands on him, God smote the king so that he had to call on the man of God to pray for him. Then he tried to reward the prophet, but the courageous preacher would have none of it; God had ordered him to return home after giving his message, and so for home he started.

So far, so good. A revival has started! God has made bare his arm and has found a faithful witness in an evil day. But the story takes a turn, and I marvel that we have not made more of it, for its warning is profound. Another prophet lived in Bethel, an old man. Maybe he had grown prosperous in that rich, apostate age by playing politics and trimming his sails to the popular breeze. I do not know. Anyway, his sons brought him word of this new prophet who had suddenly broken upon the scene. It was very exciting. A new preacher has come to town, rebuking the king himself, and the power of God is with him. Did it make the old prophet jealous? Or did it rekindle memories of a better day in his own life before he became a sycophant? Whether from jealousy or admiration, he overtook the new prophet and invited him to his house.

At first, the man of God stuck to his divine orders and refused. Then the subtle trickery comes out. "I am a prophet, too," the old man replies, "and I've had later word from the Lord and it will be all right for you to visit with me." The man of God yielded, and the rest of the story is tragedy. On his way home a lion slays him and his mission that began so nobly ends in disgrace; and Jeroboam, doubtless hearing of the preacher's fall, takes up his old ways again.

Here is a warning to the preacher who has had a commission from the Most High. Beware of these prophets who will beset you with later information from heaven. Many a revival has begun with demonstration of the Spirit and of power. The mighty have been rebuked, judgment has fallen on iniquity, and sinners have come to repentance. But Satan is not asleep. Somewhere he gets hold of another prophet who has been taking it easy and does not like this commotion because it shows him up. He advises the man of God not to be so rigid and harsh in his interpretation of the divine orders. "Let up a little. You cannot keep up such a stern program. Have dinner with me and let us be good fellows." The preacher decides that maybe he has been a bit too Puritanical. After all, we must be human. So he lets down and accepts second-hand guidance from the prophet of Bethel. The revival ends, God disapproves him, and all the Jeroboams who had been brought to repentance go back to their old ways. Instead of being an agent of revival, he ends a party to greater apostasy.

Abraham's servant, after he had found Rebekah, was urged to remain ten days. But he did not forget his instructions. "Hinder me not, seeing the Lord hath prospered my way" was his rejoinder. Would that this prophet from Judah had so kept his wits with him. Hospitality is a blessed thing, but the devil can use it to our ruin. Bunyan complained that the effect of a good sermon could be spoiled by a big Sunday dinner. McCheyne came in from an innocent party, saying, "My soul must break away from these things."

If God has given you a solemn mission, give your message and then get going. Beware of these prophets of Bethel who have heard from the Lord since you have. If the Lord is running your mission, he will tell you what to do; he will not tell somebody else. There is a lion in the way for the preacher who listens to man instead of to God in the hour of his triumph. Pity the revivalist who backslides in the midst of the revival!

CHAPTER 30

"Lovest Thou Me?"

IN our Lord's interview with repentant Simon Peter by the Sea of Tiberias, let it be remembered that he made himself the issue: "Lovest thou me?"

He could have centered everything on Peter, pointed out his weaknesses, lectured him about his denial, but that was not the issue. When Elijah had his bad day under the juniper, that was an excellent opportunity for the Lord to give him a going over. Instead he fed the prophet and put him to sleep. When John the Baptist languished in prison and sent his inquiring delegation to Jesus, there was abundant ground for giving him a reproof. Instead, the Savior spoke most highly of the great preacher who was temporarily under a shadow.

With Simon Peter, Jesus made himself the issue. He did not ask, "Do you love feeding sheep?" That would be a mere professional love. It is possible to enjoy preaching as an art without having the preacher's heart. Some of us glory in how much we love church work. Of course, it is well to like what you do; but one may be church-minded without being church-hearted, missionary-minded without being missionary-hearted. There are dear souls today who take to church work just like others take to needlepoint or stamp-collecting. It is a glorified hobby, or even a chosen vocation, and yet it may not proceed from love for Christ. Now, it would seem unthinkable to speak a word against

109

such fine church loyalty and religious activity, especially when there are so many sluggards who will not work in their church at all. Yet the Word of God thunders throughout against that very sort of thing. The church at Ephesus was busy enough; doubtless there were members who "just loved church work." But they had left their first love for Christ and were commanded by Jesus himself to repent. If you told such dear souls today that they needed to repent, they would be insulted, for they imagine that they are the last people on earth who should make any change. Aren't they holding the church together? Aren't they faithful, Sunday after Sunday? But it is possible to like feeding sheep without loving Christ.

Again, Jesus did not ask Peter, "Do you love sheep?" That is better than to love feeding sheep. Someone has said, "It is not enough to love to preach: you must love the people to whom you preach." True. And an awful lot of preaching misses the mark because it proceeds from love of preaching, not love of people. But even this is not enough. It is better, but it is not enough. It warms up the professional but still it can be only sentimental love. It will make the minister popular and likeable and put heart into what he says, but human love for humans is not sufficient for the work of God. Here, again, there are dear people working faithfully in religious duties, in missions, Sunday schools, children's work who really love those to whom they minister, but feeding sheep for Christ must proceed from a still higher source than man's love for man.

Jesus asked Peter, "Lovest thou me?" That is not professional or sentimental, but spiritual love. It is the love of God shed abroad in our hearts by the Holy Spirit as we trust Christ and yield to him. We must begin with love for Christ; then we will love others because we love him. The Philippian jailer cared nothing about the sufferings of Paul and Silas until he knew Christ; then he washed the stripes of his prisoners. We do not arrive at loving Christ by loving his people or his work. We cannot truly love either his people or his work until by a work of grace we love him. We cannot make ourselves love him, but we can trust him and yield to him, and the Spirit of God will create in us love for Christ. And we shall love the sheep and love feeding them because we love the Shepherd.

To obtain additional copies of this book, and to see a list of
other great Christian titles, including more by
Vance Havner, visit our web site:
www.KingsleyPress.com

49591149R00063

Made in the USA
Lexington, KY
22 August 2019